STARTERS ACTIVITIES

Clay

Macdonald Educational

About Starters Activities

These books cover a variety of activities for children at school or at home. The projects with their step-by-step illustrations, require the minimum of help from teachers or parents. Most of the words in the text will be in the reading vocabulary of the majority of young readers. Word and sentence length have also been carefully controlled. Extra information and more complex activities are included at the end of each book. Where possible, the child is free to invent and experiment on his own, but concise instructions are given wherever necessary. Teachers and experts have been consulted on the content and accuracy of these books.

Illustrated by: Belinda Lyon
Managing Editor: Su Swallow
Editor: Jennifer Vaughan
Production: Stephen Pawley, Rosemary Bishop

Reading consultant: Donald Moyle, author of *The Teaching of Reading* and senior lecturer in education at Edge Hill College of Education

Chairman, teacher advisory panel: F. F. Blackwell, director of the primary extension programme, National Council for Educational Technology

Teacher panel: Stephanie Connell, Sally Chaplin

Colour reproduction by:
Colourcraftsmen Limited

ISBN 0 356 04396 7

Made and printed in Great Britain by:
Adams Bros. and Shardlow Ltd, Leicester

Filmsetting by:
Layton-Sun Limited

First published in 1973 by
Macdonald and Company
(Publishers) Limited
St Giles House
49-50 Poland Street
London W1

Contents

You can make
these things from clay.

Clay is soft.
Try making different shapes.
Bang the clay flat.

Pots and baskets

These pots and baskets
are made from clay.

Roll the clay out like this.
Coil it round to make a pot.

Press the clay together
with your fingers.
Make the pot tall.
Smooth the pot inside.

Let the clay dry.
Then paint it in bright colours.

This is another way of making pots.
Make a ball of clay.
Press a hole in it with your thumbs.

Pinch the clay to make a pot.
When it is dry you can paint it.

Writing on clay

Long ago, people wrote on clay.

Roll out some soft clay.

Try writing on it. Use a thin stick.

Patterns in clay

Try pressing these things into clay.
Use these things
to make patterns in soft clay.

Make patterns
with your fingers and thumbs.

Make patterns on your pots
with a stick.

Clay heads

You can make a head from clay.
Press the clay into a ball.

Pull and push the clay to
make a nose.
Make ears.
What can you use to make eyes?

Here are all kinds of heads.
When the clay is dry
glue some hair on to them.
Use wool or string for hair.

Clay animals

Try making animals.
The hedgehog is made
with clay and pine needles.

hedgehog

All these
animals have been made
with clay.

Tiles

Try making a clay tile.
Roll the clay out. Wait till it is dry.
Then paint it.

Here are some things
to press into tiles.
Press them into the tiles.
Then let the tiles dry out.

Make many little clay tiles.
Let them dry out.
Paint them bright colours.
Make patterns with them like this.

A model street

Make a model of your street.
Put cars and buses
in the street.

Clay words

clay
(page 1)

pot
(page 3)

basket
(page 3)

coil
(page 4)

paint
(page 6)

write
(page 9)

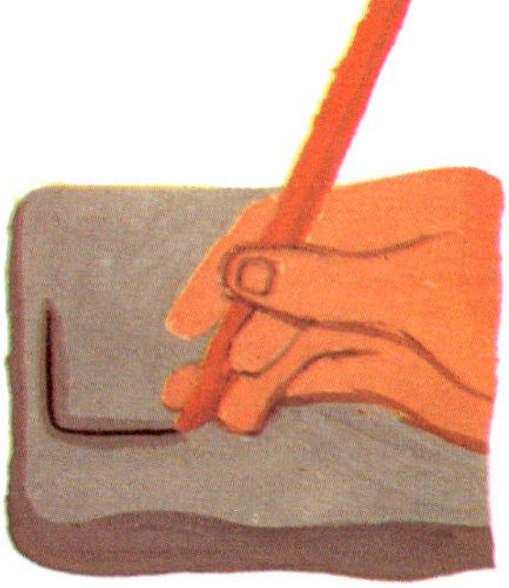

pattern
(page 10)

head
(page 13)

wool
(page 15)

hedge-
hog
(page 16)

pine
needles
(page 16)

lentils
(page 19)

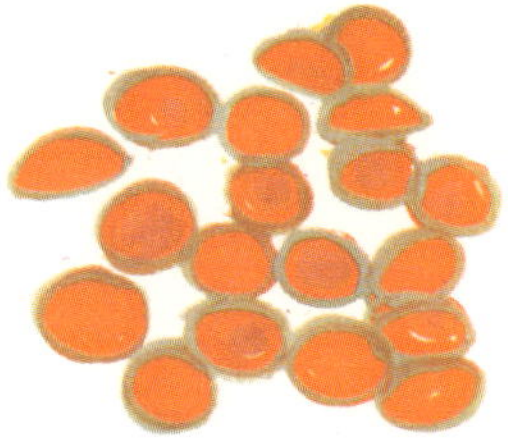

seeds
(page 19)

car
(page 21)

bus
(page 21)

Remember

Clay can make things
very dirty.
Put newspaper on the table
you are using.
Wipe everything clean
when you have finished.

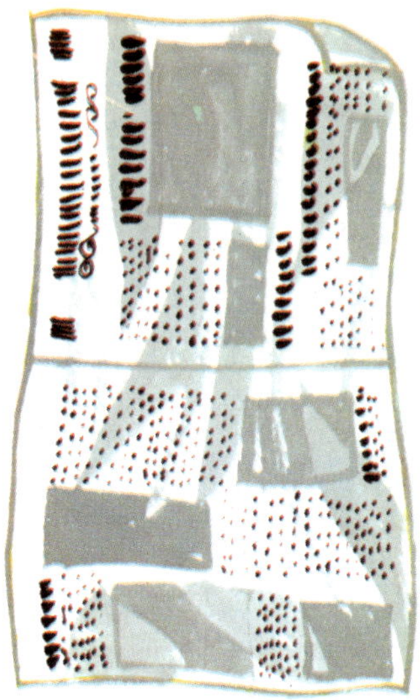

How clay is used

Most cups and plates
are made from clay.
The clay is baked to
make it hard.
Bricks are made of clay too.
Try looking for things
which are made
of clay.

Some harder projects

Clay beads

Try making clay beads. Make little balls of clay, and make a hole through the middle of each one with a thick nail or a matchstick. Then let the clay dry out, or bake it in a potter's kiln if that is possible. Some modern makes of clay are specially made so that they are quite hard and strong when dry, and do not need firing.

Clay badges

Make badges from clay. Roll the clay out until it is quite thin. Cut out the shape of badge you want. Let the shape dry, or have it baked in a kiln. Then paint the pattern you want on to the badge and fasten a safety pin to the back of it. You can use sticky tape for this, or better, a small strip of cloth and some very strong glue. Use the safety pin to fasten the badge to your clothes. You might paint clear varnish over the front of the badge if you want the paint to stay on it for a long time.

A hedgehog

Make a clay hedgehog with a hollowed-out back, like a small bowl. It is really best to bake this in a kiln and then it will last you for a long time. When it has been baked, or it has dried out, fill the hollow back of your hedgehog with a soil or potting compost. Now scatter some grass seeds into the soil and water them. Keep the soil in the hedgehog damp, but not too wet, and the grass seeds will soon grow. Your hedgehog will have green spines. Try growing mustard and cress or candytuft instead of grass.

Some harder projects

Moulds

Use clay to help you to make a picture. You will need a round tin lid or pastry cutter, some soft clay, some stiff paper and plaster of Paris. Roll the clay out until it is flat and about 3 centimetres thick. Cut out a circle in the clay with the pastry cutter or tin lid. Find some nuts, leaves or fruit and press them into the piece of clay. Leaves should be pressed face upwards so that all the marks of the veins will show up in the clay. Now take the things you have pressed into the clay out of it so that you can see the patterns they have made. Paint over the clay with grease. Next, make a collar of paper about 6 centimetres wide and fix it around the clay with paper clips or sticky tape. This should make a sort of cup, with the clay lying at the bottom of the cup, and the paper standing up around it. Ask someone to mix the plaster of Paris for you now, and quickly pour it into the cup. Very soon it will be dry. Take the plaster away from the clay, and you will find that there is a picture of the fruit and leaves from the clay on the plaster. You might want to paint this and keep it as a picture.